From ZERO to HERO

A Winning Formula to Succeed in Business & Life

Interior Design: B.O.Y. Enterprises, Inc.

ISBN: 978-1-7338051-7-9

Printed in the United States.

From ZERO to HERO

A winning formula to succeed in Business & Life

By Veronica Abisay

Table of Contents

Formula to Succeed in Business and Life.

To operate in a higher dimension, you must be willing to learn and grow every day.

INTRODUCTION

According to my background and experience, I am not deserving of this title or label "Hero." I grew up in a middle-class family. My mom and dad worked hard to make sure all their children are able to get the education they deserved. I still remember their conversations. They would say, "We would rather skip a meal in order for these children to not miss school just because we did not pay their school fees on time." They truly believed in our future and you could see their love towards us from their actions and words, which were extremely amazing.

God blessed my parents with 4 children, three girls and one boy. I grew up in a family that loved God. Every Sunday my dad would wake us up early in the morning. He knocked on our doors and told everyone to get up and get ready for church. That was our routine every Sunday and we knew that, nobody will miss church unless you're sick. This routine cemented into my mind very well that Sunday was not a day to play game with my dad at all. Let me tell you, I caught this formula for myself. If I wanted to impress my dad, I would have to prepare everything on Saturday night before I go to sleep so it become easier when I woke up on Sunday morning. I must say, it wasn't easy for my siblings, they didn't like to get up early on Sunday morning. So, as a first born, I had to make sure I helped themso we could leave the house on time.

Another good thing I liked from my parents, I never seen them speaking curse words, or fighting in front of my eyes. I didn't know how they managed that at that time, but as I grew older, I realized, they had the ability to control themselves not to show their emotions to their kids or even outsiders. If they had anything to discuss or challenge one another, they would wait until we fell asleep or they would step out for a short walk.

I watched and observed their moves very closely without them knowing.

I really admired what I saw, and I decided I would copy that lifestyle. Until today, I have come to realize as a grown-up woman, experience can be a good teacher, there are so many powerful lessons you can learn through experiences. Nobody taught me not to underestimate people, but through the lifestyle of my parents, I learned it is very important to respect everyone because you don't know what tomorrow will bring to you. I remember when they were telling me, "You don't know! Maybe the person you underestimate today, tomorrow will be a person to help you." They told me to treat all people with a dignity. I thank them for that!

Also, I learned another important thing about money. Money is good and is not evil. Money will buy me things and make life easier if I manage it very well. Also, they taught me that money will never buy happiness, so I do not need to let money control or change my attitude towards people. I cannot list everything from them as a child. There was so much love and peace in the house that you couldn't see any weakness from my parents. I believe no one is perfect. I also believe that everyone of us, we have two sides of our reality and that reality is, we have one side that shows our weakness and the other side shows our strength. It doesn't matter who you are, that's who we are. That's the reason God wants us not to depend on our own understanding instead depend fully on God. Love Him and love one another with all of our heart.

2 Corinthians 12:9 says, "and he said unto me, my grace is sufficient for thee, for my strength is made perfect in weakness. Most gladly therefore will I rather glory in my infirmities, that the power of Christ may rest upon me."

You see! God knows we have our weakness side. Sometimes we do not use good judgement or make good choices. He knows that, and there are so many scriptures in the Bible speak about weakness. If you have time, you can go through these scriptures I came across. These scriptures will expose you to the truth about how weak we are as human beings. Isaiah 41:10, Philippians 4:13, 2 Corinthians 12:10, Isaiah 40:28-31, Romans

12:2, 2 Timothy 1:7, Ephesians 6:10, Hebrews 13:5, Romans 15:13, Act 1:8, Hebrews 4:16.

This proved to me that, if everyone has weakness, it means my parents also had and still have their own weaknesses,but I really admired the way they handled it. For me not being able to notice it at that age, was a big lesson. I salute them! That's all I can say.

I remember one night in 1990, my dad came home completely changed. I was 10 years old. I grew up seeing my father joking and laughing with everyone. When he was home, everyone would notice that he was home. I used to like the way he turned the music up high and sang along. My dad loves to sing till today. But guess what? That day my dad came home and went straight to the refrigerator. We had leftover foods and drinks that were never opened. Then I saw him take all the alcohol drinks outside and put them in the trash. I was asking myself, "What is going on with my dad?" Anyway, he began to clean the refrigerator, kitchen area, and arranged things in the kitchen. It was around 9:30 pm. When my mom came back home, somebody had already told her what was going on. She got inside and started a conversation with my dad. I heard mother ask dad this question, "What happened to you?" As I was there sitting on the couch, I remember, he replied back to her and said,

"Oh! Something amazing happened to me today!" He began explaining! "I heard a small voice inside me telling me to go look for the people of God who believe in Jesus Christ. So, I dressed well and left the house to obey that voice which led me to one church not far from here. I sat down and listened to their teachings. As a preacher took the pulpit and start to teach, I started to feel guilty of my sin. I felt tears streaming down my face. After the preacher finished, I asked one of the church's leaders to give me a moment so I can speak with the Pastor. They agreed with me. After a few minutes he came shake hands with me. We sat down and I shared my story with him of how I ended up there. I was happy because he understood very well what I was trying to tell him. He told me God had sent me there for a purpose. So, he prayed for me and led me to Christ through "salvation prayer". After he finished, I asked if He could go home with me, so he can pray for my family and see where I live. In case of anything he will know where to find me, the good thing the church and our house was not far from each other, so it was a very simple move. He liked the idea and we left the church and headed to our house."

When it comes to my mom, and how she got saved, it was the same year but a different month. After seeing my dad's transformation from being a normal Christian to a believer of Jesus Christ, she decided to give her life to Jesus too. It was amazing to see the whole family surrender their life completely to Jesus and allow God to lead their steps. One week after, I saw dad came home with the wall frame decorated with this scripture

"As for me and my house, we will serve the Lord" (Joshua 24:15).

Together, they are serving the Lord. My dad as a pastor, and my mom as minister. They're always telling me, "Veronica, no one can replace the love we have for God." I am so very proud of them for their efforts, love, knowledge, and wisdom they imparted in my life. They taught me how to love God and hold God's commandments at a very early age. It's truly amazing. I cannot thank them enough, but I pray to God that He gives us more years to live so we can celebrate the fruits of their hard work. That's how my relationship with God began too.

Proverbs 22:6 says, "Start children off on the way they should go, and even when they are old they will not turn from it."

This is a powerful scripture. I practice this scripture with my own kids. I don't know what to tell you! But I see it manifesting itself to them and I know I will see more than what I see now. My job is both to feeding them with the knowledge of God and staying on top of their education. I'm a believer that when you teach your children well, one day when they grow up, they will be able to stand tall and be so proud of what they own and hold. I know this will give them confidence that no one can take it away from them.

Entrepreneur life

I finished my school years, then attended college. When I was almost finished with college, a job opportunity knocked on my door and I accepted. I was so happy; everyone knows the joy you felt when you got your first job. I was super excited! Not only me but also my parents.

My mom had a good job, so she was able to take care of us by herself plus, the income from my dad who was working for himself as an entrepreneur and a small business owner you can see life was OK.

As an entrepreneur he was able to manage his time right. Most of the time my dad was available for us. Did I mention that he was so strict? Yes, he was! He was not allowing us to go everywhere we wanted to go or invite anybody we wanted to invite to our house, unless he knew them, and he was around. Anyway, during the time of my college, I was already an entrepreneur. I was buying cookies at a wholesale price from suppliers and sold them at a retail price at my parent's shop. It was an amazing idea I came up with to "buy and sell cookies." I decided to buy instead of making myself. First of all, I did not want to waste any minutes trying to figure out how to make it myself, when I knew where I could find them for a wholesale price. Second, I had a thought that if I don't do it now somebody else will come and do it before me. The opportunity for me to make money would have been gone just like that. Third, I didn't want my cookie business to interfere with my school.

The cookie business expanded from selling 20 cookies a day to 200, then to 350. There was a time I was selling 500 cookies a day. But listen! You have to know this, there is nothing gained or achieved easily, you will have to put 100% of your effort to see the good results in whatever you are doing. Also, as an entrepreneur, you must be ready to pay the price, this business trained me to fall in the real world of entrepreneurship apart from watching my dad. There was a time I was staying late at my parent's shop to make sure I sold the last cookie, because every day I had to bring fresh cookies to the shop. I had to press hard to make sure I didn't go back home with a batch of cookies in my hand lol. Every day except Sunday, I had to wake up 4:30 am to go pick up cookies from my wonderful supplier. I don't know if she would remember me today if I went to her and asked her.

I realized in order for me to sell many cookies, the cookies had to reach the shop around 6:00 am, because those cookies were good enough to eat for breakfast. Oh the cookies were soft, fluffy, and delicious! Because I loved what I was doing, I decided to work 6 days a week for my cookie business to be where I wanted to be. As an entrepreneur, you always have a choice to refuse to be a loser and set your mind to overcome any obstacles and challenges that come your way. Having a winning attitude is the key for an entrepreneur to develop a muscle of climbing high. Make no excuses, love what you do, set goals high, and monitor progress. That's how you can continue to win in this game. There will be people here and there trying to come to you and push their opinions, advice, or agendas to look better than yours. Please don't be quick to consider them as a conclusion unless you have done your own research and you have given yourself time to meditate and ask God what your next move is.

Let me tell you, you are the one who knows what you want in your business and life. You know your goals, so you have to have the final say. You must learn to be strong and bold in all seasons. Be confident in what you believe, put the power of a winning attitude to work. This attitude is more than just saying you want to win.

If anyone is telling you that you cannot make it or trying to make you think your dreams are impossible due to their reflection of their limited mindset, always ignore them. You just focus on your goals. If you do this, you will see the positive results in your business. God will provide for you and go before you to open every closed door.

That was the beginning of my journey to becoming an entrepreneur. I was not afraid about taking risk for a good cause. I started to believe in myself more than anybody could believe in me. I set up my goals and started to work hard towards my goals and saved money. Look! Because I had two reliable sources of income which were coming from cookie business, and my new job (IT Support), life was so good for me. I was able to support my parents when the need arose, also support my dad's church by giving my tenth and offering faithfully. I continued to spend time to create ideas and find a way to execute them. In the process of creating ideas, I found out there was a need of a financial support in the community I was living in with my parents. I decided I would open a micro finance company with my saved money and my retirement to help my community to fight against poverty and the same time to build a business.

My passion always has been to empower women at all levels, so I had to talk to my dad to allow me to work with women in his church. He agreed and that's when I started my first company "Govas." I put the people in position, and we started to work side by side in unity and love. The word spread; many women came and asked for our services. We were able to serve those who were in the community and outside our community. We created a fair system that was easily to be accessible to any woman. It was an honor for me to serve those women.

So, listen my friends, when I speak about entrepreneurship, I really know what it takes to be an entrepreneur. I am the type of a person that likes to search for opportunities. When I find them, I will try to use them very well unless they weren't meant for me lol! I trained myself at a very young age to be independent financially and bring solutions to every challenge I face, no matter big or small. Also, believing in myself and putting God at the center has been my weapon since when I was younger until today.

Govas on Mission in Africa/Tanzania

Dreams work if you work.

This is my message to entrepreneurs or anyone thinking about jumping into this entrepreneurship journey. First of all, it is my belief that everyone has a gift(s), talent(s), or whatever you will like to call it. You can find this in the book of Romans 12:6,

"We have different gifts, according to the grace given to each of us. If your gift is prophesying, then prophecy in accordance with your[a] faith; 7 if it is serving, then serve; if it is teaching, then teach; 8 if it is to encourage, then give encouragement; if it is giving, then give generously; if it is to lead,[b] do it diligently; if it is to show mercy, do it cheerfully."

But in order for you to see the fruits of your gifts or talents you have to make the decision that you're going to work on it.

But how are you going to work on it? That's the question I get everywhere I go to speak about entrepreneurship, so today I am going to share with you my tips that will help you to create the business from your gifts. When you consider these tips, you will start to see the possibility of making your dreams come true.

1. What is your passion? What is your gift? Give yourself time to think, then begin to write every idea that comes in your mind on paper, and then right down the resources needed to make it happen. Ok?
2. Act on it. You can only see results when you act. So, get into overcoming business like Moses in the Bible and begin to take the first step at creating a new business, project or building the life you want.one step at a time!
3. Set your goals. Try to make sure your goals are clear and realistic. Understand the total cost of the project or business you want to do. And always remember, before you pursue a new business opportunity, you have to map out the total investment, this will give

you a clear picture of what to expect.

4. Be full-time ONLY when the business has kicked off, meanwhile you can find another way to access the money you need while your business grows.
5. Continue to be creative. Creativity and entrepreneurship go hand-in-hand and creativity is an essential tool for any entrepreneur to manage a business quicker and move business to the next level. The entrepreneurs who really thrive and succeed are the ones who can use their creativity over and over.
6. Be positive. Don't doubt yourself, instead be inspired to be the best. Learn about the challenges, overcome and allow the best practices.
7. Surround yourself with the right type of people. The people who will uplift you and make you believe in yourself. It is your responsibility as an entrepreneur to surround yourself with the best. Seek those individuals out who are living life on a different level, get out of your comfort zone, and leave the ones who restrict you to a mediocre existence. Let go and run towards your dreams. Let the ones whom you spend time with be addicted to the grind, addicted to taking action, and addicted to success.
8. Find strong mentors who having experience to guide and support you.

If you want to be successful follow those tips.

****

"SURROUND YOURSELF WITH PEOPLE WHO ARE ONLY GOING TO LIFT YOU HIGHER."

OPRAH WINFREY

****

****

"God was preparing me for great things."

****

****

“Be positive about your past and let your experience be a good teacher."

****

Formula 1

TRUST

This is the **Number #1 formula** for your breakthrough or success. But before I start, I want to ask you this question.

Can God trust you with the plans He has for you?

It's obvious that the way someone treats another person dictates the relationship between them.

Mankind is all about relationships, and relationships are built on trust, love, and mutual respect. Ask yourself, how can you trust someone who lies to you, cheats on you, lies about you, steals from you, assaults you, or disregards the things you say. All relationships are built or governed by the rules, so do not be surprised when it comes to God. He expects us to have the closeness and trust with Him. God wants us to show our genuine love towards Him, more than any relationships we have.

To acknowledge him as our Father and Creator of the whole universe and know that without Him, there's nothing we can accomplish .The Bible says, "God created us in his own image on the last day of creation." Yes, we are God's children.

Let me share with you this scripture from the book of Genesis 1:26 so you can see what bible says about humankind, "Then God said, "let us make man in our image to be like us, and let them have dominion over the fish of the sea, and the birds in the sky, over the livestock and all the wild animals, and over all the creatures that move along the ground. In the image of God He created him, male and female He created them. And God blessed them, and God said to them "Be fruitful and multiply, and fill the earth, and subdue it, and rule over the fish of the sea and over the birds of the sky, and over every living thing that move on the earth. Then God said, "Behold, I have given you every plant yielding seed that is on the surface of all the earth, and every tree which has fruits yielding seed. It shall be food for you and it was so. And God saw all that he had made and behold, it was very good, And there was evening and there was morning, the sixth day.

So, our relationship with God was planned well and was perfect in the eyes of the Father. God trusted Adam and Eve to take care of all creation.

He wanted them to rule over His creation. It is sad that the fall of man in God's perfect plan came through the Serpent (Satan) who went to the woman and deceived her, by asking "Did God really say, you must not eat from any tree in the garden?" He tried to convince Eve that God was holding back something good from her by prohibiting her from eating of the forbidden tree, and Eve became convinced of her need to "know good and evil".

The bible says the serpent was craftier than any of the wild animals the Lord has made. When the woman (Eve) saw that the tree was good for food, and that it was a delight to the eyes, and that tree was desirable to make one wise, she took from its fruits and ate, and she gave also to her husband with her, and he ate. Then, the eyes of both were open.

So, from there our relationship with God got into a major crack, God was angry with all three of them! As I go deeper studying the fall of man, I came to realize that God the Father had unfailing and unceasing love towards us despite of all the destruction the serpent caused trying to pull man away from God.

Because we have been created for the purpose, God came back with another plan, that led Him to let his beloved son, Jesus Christ to be crucified on the cross for the sin and mistakes he didn't commit, Galatians 3:13-15 says; 13 "Christ paid the price to free us from the curse that the laws in Moses' Teachings bring by becoming cursed instead of us."

Scripture says, "Everyone who is hung on a tree is cursed." 14 Christ paid the price so that the blessing promised to Abraham would come to all the people of the world through Jesus Christ and we would receive the promised Spirit through faith.

Do you see how God was committed to see the people he created in his own image not perish? This chapter must position and renew your mind to take your relationship with God our Father very seriously.

Jeremiah 1:5 says, "Before I formed you in the womb I knew you, before you were born I set you apart and appointed you as my prophet to nations." You see that!

God has a purpose with our life, and He loves us so much, the question is, can God trust you with the plans he has for you? When he gives you the task to do, will you do according to the instructions he gave or you will do on your own ways?

God trusted Adam and Eve. He provided them with everything they needed to live. Eve and Adam had been in perfect relationship and fellowship with God until they disobeyed and sinned against God. The bible says, "Then they heard the sound of the Lord God walking about in the garden, they hid themselves from the face of Jehovah God in the midst of the trees of the garden because they knew that they disobeyed and sinned against God.

What do you learn from this in our today's life?

You know being trustworthy is one of the best character traits to have.

Smart is good, but if you can't be trusted, no one will believe your smartness. Attractive personality is wonderful, but if you cannot be trusted you are nothing. If you promised somebody your kids, spouse, or friends that you will be there for them always, and one day one of them got sick and they are calling you, will they trust you to be there?

Ask yourself today, "can you really be trusted with God when all hell is breaking loose around you?" Can God trust you when Satan decides to shoot a fiery dart at your marriage, your children, your finances or your health? Can He trust you when the bank says there is no more money and you just bounced a check?

Many people treat their relationship with God that way. They wonder, can I really trust Him? Does He really have my best interest at heart? And you know the truth is, He does. Think about it, the God of the universe, creates you and me, and decides to allow us to choose Him or not to choose Him just because He wants to be loved freely by our own free will.

Some people say, if God was so loving, why wouldn't He just make us love Him and avoid the whole sin thing. God chose the loving act of giving us a free will, so that He wouldn't force anyone to do what they did not want to do.

As a believer, we need to know that when you put your trust in God, there is no need to fear. I understand that life can be difficult sometimes because we are in a battle with the devil, He really does not want us to be on the winning side of Jesus Christ. He wants us to do things that do not glorify our Father as he convinced Eve to eat the fruit from forbidden tree, so we find ourselves struggling against sin like; pride, lust, greed, boasting, and various desires.

Also, we have war against the world. The world wants to change our character and convert us to its paganism, or to its ungodly devotion to the unholy. Keep this in mind, in the battle there are all sorts of struggles, we find ourselves struggling against illness, poverty, marriage problems, job difficulties, an unsure future, and more. But there's HOPE after all these that we know our Father God who is Holy and ruler of all nations has the power to take us through and He trust us to do what He is telling us so we don't fall into the traps of our enemies .

The love of God is so big, that's why He let his only son Jesus Christ come and serve us, you can read this from John 3:16, "For God so loved the world that he gave his one and only Son, that whoever believes in him shall not perish but have eternal life." Then, He left us with the Holy Spirit to guide us, to protect us, to walk with us. That's the kind of God I really want to serve. God has to be trustworthy.

Did you know that? He has to be trustworthy, because He is truth. God has revealed his truth through His Word and through Jesus, His Son. The truth is that, He loves us very much, and wants to have a close relationship with us.

This is a question you need to keep asking yourself, when God looks at me, will He trust me in whatever dimensions He wants to take me?

I want us first to look at the spiritual realm before we jump to the real talk of money. Let us see the people in the Bible that God trusted them with the gospel and their teachings. A good example was;

— Apostle Paul—

Apostle Paul was trusted with the Gospel

1 Thessalonians 2:4; "On the contrary, we speak as those approved by God to be entrusted with the gospel. We are not trying to please people but God, who tests our hearts."

What makes one trustworthy with the gospel is having love for God and others. Have courage to share the words of God without fear with believers and unbelievers. Also, to want to know Him more by equipping themselves with the knowledge.

Again, look at Paul's Ministry in Thessalonica from (1 Thessalonians 2:1-6); You know, brothers and sisters, that our visit to you was not without results. 2 We had previously suffered and been treated outrageously in Philippi, as you know, but with the help of our God we dared to tell you his gospel in the face of strong opposition. 3 For the appeal we make does not spring from error or impure motives, nor are we trying to trick you. 4 On the contrary, we speak as those approved by God to be entrusted with the gospel. We are not trying to please people but God, who tests our hearts. 5 You know we never used flattery, nor did we put on a mask to cover up greed—God is our witness. 6 We were not looking for praise from people, not from you or anyone else, even though as apostles of Christ we could have asserted our authority.

The Effort of Paul and others accompanied him on what we call the missionary journey had not been in vain. Their efforts had really bore the fruits in Thessalonica. It was a busy city, linked to all the important cities of Macedonia.

These are the things we need to know that made Paul and Silas to be trusted with Gospel;

1. They had boldness-This is what they said; You know how badly we had been treated at Philippi just before we came to you and how much we suffered there. Yet our God gave us the courage to declare his Good News to you boldly, in spite of great opposition.

2. Speak to please God-For we speak as messengers approved by God to be entrusted with the Good News. Our purpose is to please God, not people. He alone examines the motives of our hearts.

3. Approved by God-God tried Paul and Silas and passed the test. Their approval was from God and not from any man. With the help of the Holy Spirit, they preached the word of God as it is, they walked in the light of the gospel, they were loyal to the Lord, they were not ashamed of the gospel.

4. They were aware that God sees their heart. He alone knows what our hearts think about Him and we choose to do what we're doing. Look here; 1 Thessalonians 2:4- "He alone examines the motives of our heart".

Brethren, we cannot cheat God, we have to understand, He knows our hidden thoughts. Let us try to keep our motives pure when we do His work. I have seen nowadays, many preachers or ministers of the gospel (not all of them don't get me wrong) but most of them their motive is to make money. And I always ask God in my prayer to raise apostles like the apostles of those day who will not be ashamed of the gospel and will be ready to serve God with pure motives.

Look what Paul said from the book of Romans 14:8; "If we live, it's to honor the Lord. And If we die, it's to honor the Lord. So whether we live or die, we belong to the Lord".

It is very important to know that there are things that can make us untrustworthy.

1. False teachings-We must make sure our teachings are true. Always speak the truth; do not confuse people with the false doctrines.

2. Impurity -We have to make sure our motives are clean. Paul's preaching didn't come from moral or spiritual impurity. The Bible says his motives were clean.

3. Greed-Some preachers are seeking material rewards by their works at

the expense of others. They give false hopes to gain something in a material way.

4. Trickery-Paul was not a trickster, He was much more a giver than a taker of good things.

5. Flattery-Paul was not a man pleaser., He spoke plainly and lovingly.

— Isaiah —

We serve a God that thinks about our lives, our world, and his creation on a completely different level. The Bible shows us God still calls people today to go back to Him with the message of the gospel of salvation. This is the sign of love for the fallen world. It is our great gift, privilege and honor to have Him on our side after all evils people do. He still wants to serve everyone so we can maintain a closer relationship with Him and finally see Him.

So Isaiah had the revelation from God (this will be our key verse 6:1-13)

"Then I heard the voice of the Lord saying, 'whom shall I send, and who will go for us, and I said, Here am I. Send me."

This passage gives us the background under which God called Isaiah. Isaiah was one the most well-known prophets in the Bible; He wrote 66 chapters. This is more than any other book in the Bible except the book of Psalms which has 150. Isaiah prophesied many amazing prophecies about the coming of the Messiah Jesus Christ and his suffering and His resurrection from the dead.

It was in the temple that Isaiah experienced something that would change his life. In the temple he saw an incredible vision, met the almighty God and heard the word of the Lord. The word of the Lord revealed who the Lord is and what Isaiah should do. Because the people were morally and spiritually corrupt. the first five chapters of Isaiah reveal the immorality, spiritually, adultery, and superficial worship of the people. The rich people oppressed the poor, young people stayed up late and drank all night. Isaiah seemed hopeless due to the sin and he said the whole head of the nation of Israel was injured and its whole heart afflicted.

So in this situation, Isaiah went to the temple to pray and ask God how they can get out from of this awful situation. That was when Isaiah discovered through this vision that God is reigning over all the Earth, high and exalted as the King of Kings and Lord of Lords.

It doesn't matter what we are going through, we need to learn to live by faith like Isaiah and we need to keep in mind, His love towards us is BIG.

Let's look at verse 1 one more time. "In the year that King Uzziah died, I saw the Lord seated on a throne, high and exalted and the train of his robe filled the temple." Wow, what an incredible vision! God revealed himself to Isaiahand showed himself to Isaiah that he was the living God seated on his mighty throne. The words "seated on a throne" means that God is ruling high and exalted over all the nations as the King of Kings and Lord of Lords. This vision given to Isaiah, shows that God is in sovereign control of the universe. Isaiah thought that he and his people had no hope becauseof their human situations. He thought the world was ruled by superpower nations.

Look at verse 2, "Above him were seraphim, each with six wings: With two wings they covered their faces, with two they covered their feet, and with two they were flying. 3 And they were calling to one another: "Holy, holy, holy is the Lord Almighty; the whole earth is full of his glory." 4 At the sound of their voices the doorposts and thresholds shook, and the temple was filled with smoke.

Isaiah thought the world was looking dark, but it wasn't dark to the seraphim and to God himself. "The whole world is full of his glory" means that God is not controlled by man's situation. Also, it means that God is still God no matter what goes on in earth. His love towards us is what makes Him pour His blessings towards us and keep protecting us. He is unchanging God .

It is our sin and actions that make God angry and make the world a bad place to live. Like Isaiah, we need to meet God personally to experience who He really is. Many times we limit God because of our human situations; our problems may seem endless. We say, "If only my situation was better. If only I didn't have to deal with this or that." We take our eyes off of God Almighty and fall into defeated thinking and habitual complaining and moaning. We need our spiritual eyes to be opened to see God's glory and accept that he is the sovereign Ruler of the world and that he cares for us personally. This vision that Isaiah saw helped him to go on because it led him to begin to know who God is and it also helped him to see who he was.

Look at verses 4-5, "At the sound of their voices the doorposts and thresholds shook and the temple was filled with smoke. Woe to me! I cried. I am ruined! For I am a man of unclean lips, and I live among a people of unclean lips, and my eyes have seen the King, the Lord Almighty." Not only was this vision to see God breathtaking for Isaiah and awesome, the fact that he saw who he was before God was life shaking and awesome itself. The first thing Isaiah did when he saw God was that he found himself to be a sinner and he cried tears of repentance.

When a person comes into God's presence, whether through prayer, Bible study, a message or someone's witness, he can only cry tears of repentance. "Woe to me I am ruined!" This is the beginning point of our life of faith when we realize who the God of the Bible is and when we cry tears of repentance over our sins. It is at this point when we can begin to learn humbly from God and grow to be His servant. This reminds me of when I had a personal encounter with God and the Lord began to reveal to me the glory of the fire and teach me what the "woman of Fire" means. That's where the journey began to start “woman of Fire” movement. “where I teach and empower women to ignite their fire for Jesus and inspire them to find their purpose.

Now let’s talk about money

Can God trust you in the realm of money?

First of all, you need to know,

“You do not own anything; you only manage the money and possessions that God has entrusted to you.” God does not own just ten percent, so that you’re free to spend the rest as you please. He owns it all, money and possessions, ok?

Here are the fundamental things you need to know:

1. You’re a steward of God’s asset

From the book of Proverbs 27:23-24; “Be sure you know the condition of your flocks, give careful attention to your herds; for riches do not endure forever, and a crown is not secure for all generations. In other words, possessions do not manage themselves. You must take care of your money and possessions, even if you are a king, or you will lose them. To be irresponsible with money or things is to be an unfaithful steward.

Matthew 25:15 says, “And unto one he gave five talents, to another two, and to another one; to every man according to his several ability; and straightway took his journey.”

What are we learning here is;

As long as I’m being responsible and careful with what God has entrusted me with, I’m good, and when something beyond my control happens, I know He will make a way, because it is not my problem, Alright?

2. You have the opportunity for advancement.

Matthew 25:15-28 says; "To one he gave five bags of gold, to another two bags, and to another one bag,[a] each according to his ability. Then he went on his journey. 16 The man who had received five bags of gold went at once and put his money to work and gained five bags more. 17 So also, the one with two bags of gold gained two more. 18 But the man who had received one bag went off, dug a hole in the ground and hid his master's money. 19 "After a long time the master of those servants returned and settled accounts with them. 20 The man who had received five bags of gold brought the other five. 'Master,' he said, 'you entrusted me with five bags of gold. See, I have gained five more.' 21 "His master replied, 'Well done, good and faithful servant! You have been faithful with a few things; I will put you in charge of many things. Come and share your master's happiness!' 22 "The man with two bags of gold also came. 'Master,' he said, 'you entrusted me with two bags of gold; see, I have gained two more.' 23 "His master replied, 'Well done, good and faithful servant! You have been faithful with a few things; I will put you in charge of many things. Come and share your master's happiness!" 24 "Then the man who had received one bag of gold came. 'Master,' he said, 'I knew that you are a hard man, harvesting where you have not sown and gathering where you have not scattered seed. 25 So I was afraid and went out and hid your gold in the ground. See, here is what belongs to you.' 26 "His master replied, 'You wicked, lazy servant! So you knew that I harvest where I have not sown and gather where I have not scattered seed? 27 Well then, you should have put my money on deposit with the bankers, so that when I returned I would have received it back with interest. 28 'So take the bag of gold from him and give it to the one who has ten bags. 29 For whoever has will be given more, and they will have an abundance. Whoever does not have, even what they have will be taken from them. 30 And throw that worthless servant outside, into the darkness, where there will be weeping and gnashing of teeth.'

Jesus' point is, if you're faithful with a little thing (money), God will give you more to manage. Lets say you have a job that is not pleasant, but you're faithful in that job, God will give you a more important job. God views our faithfulness in managing the money and things He entrusts to us as the practice game. Money is a "little thing" to God, although it's not to us! If we mess up in the practice game with the little thing (money), God isn't going to put us in the big game.

1 Timothy 3:1-7, we find another good example that shows how much God wants us to be a good steward, It talks about qualifications for Overseers and Deacons. Read here;

"1 Here is a trustworthy saying. Whoever aspires to be an overseer desires a noble task. 2 Now the overseer is to be above reproach, faithful to his wife, temperate, self-controlled, respectable, hospitable, able to teach, 3 not given to drunkenness, not violent but gentle, not quarrelsome, not a lover of money. 4 He must manage his own family well and see that his children obey him, and he must do so in a manner worthy of full respect. 5 If anyone does not know how to manage his own family, how can he take care of God's church? 6 He must not be a recent convert, or he may become conceited and fall under the same judgment as the devil. 7 He must also have a good reputation with outsiders, so that he will not fall into disgrace and into the devil's trap. In order for one to be entrusted with God for spiritual oversight of the souls which Jesus purchased with His blood, they need to have this requirement of (good stewardship)of households, which includes finances .If they aren't faithful with the little matter of money, they won't be faithful with the big matter of souls.

This means that, if you desire to be used with God in any areas in the body of Christ, you need to get your financial life in order. Because through our finances we are showing our trust in God. It also means that God will not bless our church or ministry with converts and solid growth unless we, the members, get our financial houses in order. If you want to advance in terms of responsibility in God's service, prove yourself faithful in money matters and the Lord will give you true riches.

Luke 16:1-13 talks about **The Parable of the Shrewd Manager.**

16 Jesus told his disciples: "There was a rich man whose manager was accused of wasting his possessions. 2 So he called him in and asked him, 'What is this I hear about you? Give an account of your management, because you cannot be manager any longer.' 3 "The manager said to himself, 'What shall I do now? My master is taking away my job. I'm not strong enough to dig, and I'm ashamed to beg— 4 I know what I'll do so that, when I lose my job here, people will welcome me into their houses.' 5 "So he called in each one of his master's debtors. He asked the first, 'How much do you owe my master?'6 "'Nine hundred gallons[a] of olive oil,' he replied. "The manager told him, 'Take your bill, sit down quickly, and make it four hundred and fifty.' 7 "Then he asked the second, 'And how much do you owe?' "'A thousand bushels[b] of wheat,' he replied. "He told him, 'Take your bill and make it eight hundred.' 8 "The master commended the dishonest manager because he had acted shrewdly. For the people of this world are more shrewd in dealing with their own kind than are the people of the light. 9 I tell you, use worldly wealth to gain friends for yourselves, so that when it is gone, you will be welcomed into eternal dwellings. 10 "Whoever can be trusted with very little can also be trusted with much, and whoever is dishonest with very little will also be dishonest with much. 11 So if you have not been trustworthy in handling worldly wealth, who will trust you with true riches? 12 And if you have not been trustworthy with someone else's property, who will give you property of your own?" Jesus is encouraging His followers (me and you) today to be generous with our wealth. Also, He is drawing a contrast between the "sons of the world" (unbelievers) and the "sons of light" (believers).

The word says; "Unbelievers are wiser in the things of this world than believers. We have to know that wealth is not inherently evil, but the love of money can lead to all sorts of sin." (1 Timothy 6:10)

And this parable made it clear that Jesus did not say that believers should gain wealth unrighteously and be generous with it. He wants His followers to be just, righteous stewards.

But, I'm often shocked by the way that many churches fail to teach their members to respect both their own and others' property. That's why we are ending up having the Christians who are suffering from the bondage of debts and poverty. God wants to use our finances to teach us to trust him, to become trustworthy, to prove His love for us, to guide us, and to meet our needs. So now let us start teaching one another and remind ourselves to be responsible for the things that God has blessed us before His return.

If we understand the principle that everything we own is a gift from God, then we will realize that God is the owner of everything and that we are His stewards. As such, we are to use the master's resources to further the Master's goals.

Tips to Handle Money in God's way

- Be Faithful in the little things. Don't wait until you get fortune.
- Handling your money seriously. Decide to be faithful in the little things that you have.
- Empower yourself to say no to unnecessary money expenses.
- Learn to value the money
- Don't be consumed with wanting more wealth of this world instead seek first the kingdom of God.

Can you be trusted?

Do you know when people trust you, they will count on your actions and advice to help them manage their life and business. So as an Entrepreneur and business owner, to know how to create and keep great client relationships is key to successful business. Trust opens the door for opportunities, collaboration, and long-term connection with your potential clients. You must ensure that environments of trust are authentically established where people or clients can have confidence with you.

All clients want to trust their business partners or providers, but are sometimes hesitant because they don't see these things from you. By practicing the Five keys of Trust; Be a good listener, available, dependable, accountable, and reasonable, you will establish a strong bond required in all successful client relationships.

Key #1. Availability.

Be available- You've got to help your clients fall in love with your business. No one trusts a person who doesn't show interest in their concerns.

Supply your clients with what they want, when they want it, and how they want it, in a friendly and professional way. Clients will be likely to recommend your services or products to their connections based on your availability when they need you.

Schedule periodic calls with your clients to share updates about how things are going and ask how happy they are with your services on a scale from 1-10, 10 being the best. If they don't give you a 10, do not ask why but ask them this question; what it would take to make it a 10? If they give you 10, ask what they particularly appreciate. You see!

How well you communicate with sincere effort to upgrade what the client wants is a key measure by which customers gauge whether you care.

Key #2. Be a good listener

It's a great opportunity for your brand to outshine the competition if you have an ear to listen. The best client service and company improvement comes from people listening to other people.

Whether by conducting surveys, or maybe they're asking you questions about products or service you sell. You have to be able to listen your client's needs. Listening in and using the feedback constructively can have positive results for your client's experience, which will lead you to more repeating business, referrals, and word-of-mouth marketing. But it only works if you are listening to the right cues.

Key #3. Dependable.

Being dependable means being able to be counted on or relied upon. When it comes to the business, it requires both an honest assessment of clients' goals and follow-through. You need to show your clients that you are dependable and that your client matters by building trust and honesty. Have the confidence to say to your client "I'm going to do something," and you do it. Also, have a confidence to say to your staff, "I'm going to improve the "specific" department," and you do it.

Key #4. Be Accountable

Be willing to do everything in your power to succeed convincingly. Put your word and reputation on the line.

Think customers first, you need to know your clients. Commit to knowing your client's business. If they are wholesale clients ask them questions to know the strategy and plans, if they are retailers ask them what are they looking for? What can the company solve for them? That's how you stay focused and hold yourself accountable. This applies to your staff too, commit to knowing them and their limits. Keep in mind, if you overload your team, sooner or later the collapse will appear. Eventually, productivity levels will decrease dramatically before you even realize. Be careful, because at the end, you're going to be accountable and you may receive a bad reputation.

Key #5. Be Reasonable

Customers often expect more than you can do because they don't know what to expect from you. Always remain clear-minded to see the big picture, it's possible to manage their expectations. First, assess the situation, offer guidance, and deliver what you can and keep them happy. That's the best way.

Trust the Lord

In order to have a successful life, you must trust in the Lord. God's will is what is best for you. There will be times when you do not understand why things are happening in your life, but remember God is always on your side trying to teach you and protect you.

There will be times in your life when no one will think that you are going in the right direction with your life or business, but no one can stop God's anointing. If he gave you the idea, vision, or plan for your business, he will bless it. Stay faithful and focused. When you think you have nowhere to lean, just trust the Master who is Jesus.

There are scriptures that will keep you grounded to the Lord;

Proverbs 3:5-6 "Trust in the Lord with all your heart and lean not on your own understanding; in all your ways submit to him and He will make your path straight."

Psalms 37:5 "commit your way to the Lord, trust also in Him, and He shall bring it to pass"

Philippians 4:6 "Do not be anxious about anything, but in everything, by prayer and petition, with thanksgiving, present your requests to God."

Joshua 1:9 "Have I not commanded you? Be strong and courageous. Do not be terrified; do not be discouraged, for the LORD your God will be with you wherever you go."

1 Timothy 1:7 "God has not given me a spirit of fear, butof power, love and sound mind."

Habakkuk 2:3 "But these things I plan won't happen right away. Slowly, steadily, surely, the time approaches when the vision will be fulfilled. If it seems slow, do not despair, for these things will surely come to pass. Just be patient! They will not be overdue a single day."

****

"Everything we own is a gift from God"

****

****

“We were created to dominate!”

****

Formula 2

Obedience

Formula Number #2 is Obedience to God

Do you want to succeed in life through God? Then you must be obedient to God, because He is pleased with our "**obedience**" towards Him. When he tells us to do something and we do exactly as He instructed without making any excuses to Him or to ourselves, that is called "obedience." Obedience is the fruit of faith; you believe and take it the way it is no matter what. You obey God for what he said concerning your life, your finances, your marriage, your children, or your health and know that "God has said."

That was what Eve was supposed to do when the serpent came to convince her to eat the fruit from the forbidden tree. We saw from the scripture above; she wasn't supposed to compromise with Satan even for a single second. Eve only needed to know that God had forbidden the fruit of this tree. As I was reading this chapter and tried to put myself into Eve's shoes, I believe Eve was asking herself why the fruit was forbidden? Today, you and I ask ourselves so many questions when things don't go our way, we ask 'Why God?' 'Why?' And sometimes complain. What we should be asking God is,

"What are you trying to teach me Lord?"

I came to realize that God desires from us the 'obedience of faith.' The obedience of faith is based on our faith in God, not on our own understanding of why God calls one thing good and another evil.

I know this will be the next question you ask; Did Eve trust God? But we do not need to point fingers at her, how foolish she was not trusting God and disobeying His command, but we have to remember that Eve's temptation is still with us and her sin is routinely repeating without us knowing. We say we want to obey God, but we still want to understand why we should obey him. We want to understand why God has commanded some things and prohibited others. When we fail to understand the reason, as quick and easily as Eve, we refuse God's commandment.

I love this scripture, "**we cannot understand God's plan.**" From the book of Ecclesiastes 8:16-17, "I tried to understand all that happens on earth. I saw how busy people are working day and night and hardly ever sleeping. I also saw all that God has done. Nobody can understand what God does here on earth. No matter how hard people try to understand it, they cannot. Even if wise people say they understand they cannot, no one can really understand it."

I know you can ask God questions and He will answer but you cannot understand His work and we are not supposed to. Our work is to OBEY, that means trusting him and doing what He is telling us to do is the way to go. He is a God of miracles, signs, and wonders. He will do accordingly to His wish.

Isaiah 55:8-9 says; "for my thoughts are not your thoughts, neither are your ways my ways, declares the Lord, for as the heavens are higher than the earth, so are my ways higher than your ways and my thoughts than your thoughts

Let us read the book of genesis 12:1-20 to see another good example of a person who obeyed God and he is called "the friend of God"

Genesis 12:1 The LORD told Abram, "**You are to leave your land, your**

relatives, and your father's house and go to the land that I'm going to show you. 2 I'll make a great nation of your descendants, I'll bless you, and I'll make your reputation great, so that you will be a blessing. 3 I'll bless those who bless you, but I'll curse the one who curses you, and through you all the people of the earth will be blessed." 4 So Abram left there, as the LORD had directed him, and Lot accompanied him. Abram was 75 years old when he left Haran. 5 Abram took his wife Sarai, his nephew Lot, all the possessions they had accumulated, and the servants he had acquired while living in Haran. Then they set out to go to the land of Canaan. When they arrived in the land of Canaan, 6 Abram traveled through the land to the place called Shechem, as far as the oak of Moreh. At that time the Canaanites were in the land. 7 Then the LORD appeared to Abram and said, "I'll give this land to your descendants." So Abram built an altar to the LORD, who had appeared to him. 8 From there Abram traveled on to the hill country east of Bethel and set up his tent, with Bethel on the west and Ai on the east. There he built an altar to the LORD and called on the name of the LORD. 9 Then Abram traveled on, continuing into the Negev.

Abram and Sarai in Egypt

10 There was a famine in the land, so Abram went down to Egypt to live because the famine was so severe. 11 When he was about to enter Egypt, he told his wife Sarai, "Look, I'm aware that you're a beautiful woman. 12 When the Egyptians see you, they will say, 'She is his wife.' Then they'll kill me, but allow you to live. 13 Please say that you are my sister, so things will go well for me for your sake. That way, you'll be saving my life." 14 As Abram was entering Egypt, the Egyptians noticed how beautiful Sarai was. 15 When Pharaoh's officials saw her, they brought her to the attention of Pharaoh and took the woman to Pharaoh's palace. 16 He treated Abram well because of her, so Abram acquired sheep, oxen, male and female donkeys, male and female servants, and camels. 17 But the LORD afflicted Pharaoh and his household with severe plagues because of Sarai, Abram's wife. 18 Pharaoh summoned Abram and asked, "What have you

done to me! Why didn't you tell me that she was your wife? 19 Why did you say, 'She is my sister,' so that I took her as a wife for myself? Now, here is your wife! Take her and get out!" 20 So Pharaoh assigned men to Abram, and they escorted him, his wife, and all that he had out of the country.

Let us continue to look up the life of Abraham and The Sacrifice of Isaac **Genesis 22:1-19**

1 After these things God tested Abraham and said to him, "Abraham!" And he said, "Here I am." 2 He said, "Take your son, your only son Isaac, whom you love, and go to the land of Moriah, and offer him there as a burnt offering on one of the mountains of which I shall tell you." 3 So Abraham rose early in the morning, saddled his donkey, and took two of his young men with him, and his son Isaac. And he cut the wood for the burnt offering and arose and went to the place of which God had told him. 4 On the third day Abraham lifted up his eyes and saw the place from afar. 5 Then Abraham said to his young men, "Stay here with the donkey; I and the boy[a] will go over there and worship and come again to you." 6 And Abraham took the wood of the burnt offering and laid it on Isaac his son. And he took in his hand the fire and the knife. So they went both of them together. 7 And Isaac said to his father Abraham, "My father!" And he said, "Here I am, my son." He said, "Behold, the fire and the wood, but where is the lamb for a burnt offering?" 8 Abraham said, "God will provide for himself the lamb for a burnt offering, my son." So they went both of them together. 9 When they came to the place of which God had told him, Abraham built the altar there and laid the wood in order and bound Isaac his son and laid him on the altar, on top of the wood. 10 Then Abraham reached out his hand and took the knife to slaughter his son. 11 But the angel of the Lord called to him from heaven and said, "Abraham, Abraham!" And he said, "Here I am." 12 He said, "Do not lay your hand on the boy or do anything to him, for now I know that you fear God, seeing you have not withheld your son, your only son, from me." 13 And Abraham lifted up his eyes and looked, and behold,

behind him was a ram, caught in a thicket by his horns. And Abraham went and took the ram and offered it up as a burnt offering instead of his son.

14 So Abraham called the name of that place, "The Lordwill provide";[b] as it is said to this day, "On the mount of the Lord it shall be provided."[c] 15 And the angel of the Lord called to Abraham a second time from heaven 16 and said, "By myself I have sworn, declares the Lord, because you have done this and have not withheld your son, your only son, 17 I will surely bless you, and I will surely multiply your offspring as the stars of heaven and as the sand that is on the seashore. And your offspring shall possess the gate of his[d] enemies, 18 and in your offspring shall all the nations of the earth be blessed, because you have obeyed my voice." 19 So Abraham returned to his young men, and they arose and went together to Beersheba. And Abraham lived at Beersheba.

The scripture teaches us about his faith, and his obedience to God. The bible says; Abraham tied Isaac and put him on the altar. He held the knife over Isaac. Abraham was ready to sacrifice his son. But an angel spoke to Abraham. He told Abraham not to sacrifice Isaac. Abraham had obeyed God. God loved Abraham.

Today we call him, Abraham, the Father of our Faith, He is our father in the presence of God.

What Abraham did was like what Heavenly Father did. Heavenly Father was willing to let his son, Jesus Christ, die for us. Heavenly Father and Abraham loved their sons. Jesus and Isaac loved their fathers and obeyed them. That's why Abraham was called a friend of God.

Abram, a high father, had his name changed by God to Abraham, which in Hebrew means father of multitude. God said that he would be the father of many nations.

Abraham was a very rich man and had 318 trained soldiers in his own household.

Obedience to God Brings Prosperity & Abundance-

Just look what God told Abraham! Only because he Obeyed the voice of God, and God told him, "I will be your God and bless those who bless you."

Let's read Deuteronomy 28:1-14,

This chapter opened my spiritual eyes and gave me insight.

"1 And it shall come to pass, if thou shalt hearken diligently unto the voice of the Lord thy God, to observe and to do all his commandments which I command thee this day, that the Lord thy God will set thee on high above all nations of the earth. 2 All these blessings will come on you and accompany you if you obey the Lord your God 3 You will be blessed in the city and blessed in the country. 4 The fruit of your womb will be blessed, and the crops of your land and the young of your livestock—the calves of your herds and the lambs of your flocks. 5 Your basket and your kneading trough will be blessed. 6 You will be blessed when you come in and blessed when you go out. 7 The Lord will grant that the enemies who rise up against you will be defeated before you. They will come at you from one direction but flee from you in seven. 8 The Lord will send a blessing on your barns and on everything you put your hand to. The Lord your God will bless you in the land he is giving you. 9 The Lord will establish you as his holy people, as he promised you on oath, if you keep the commands of the Lord your God and walk in obedience to him. 10 Then all the peoples on earth will see that you are called by the name of the Lord, and they will fear you. 11 The Lord will grant you abundant prosperity—in the fruit of your womb, the young of your livestock and the crops of your ground—in the land he swore to your ancestors to give you. 12 The Lord will open the heavens, the storehouse of his bounty, to send rain on your land in season and to bless all the work of your hands. You will lend to many nations but will borrow from none. 13 The Lord will make you the head, not the tail. If you pay attention to the commands of the Lord your God that I give you this day and carefully follow them,

you will always be at the top, never at the bottom. 14 Do not turn aside from any of the commands I give you today, to the right or to the left, following other gods and serving them.

WOW! How beautiful it is to be overtaken by the blessings of the Lord!

This is the basic requirement for the children of God to live anabundant life. "Obey and follow all His commands". I see many people run after them, but I like to live the kind of life where the blessings run after me as God directing them. Let me point out to you, It does not matter what God is telling you or sending your way, you have no OPTION but to obey.

Beloved, obedience is the key to prosperity not otherwise. Bible declare that whoever does not obey will have the opposite. Let'sgo back to the book of Deuteronomy 28:15-68, Moses literally lists each of those curses and these are the summary of those curses;

- You are cursed in the city and in the country.
- Your children are cursed and your crops and animals arealso cursed.
- You are cursed in your going out and coming in.
- The Lord will curse everything you set your hands to do.
- You will not have good health.
- The sky over your head will be bronze and the earth underneath iron.
- You will come at your enemies in one direction but flee in seven directions.
- Your carcass will be food for the birds.
- You will not enjoy the fruit of your labor.
- The alien will be the head, you will be the tail.
- You will never find rest and will always be anxious.
- The worst of these curses is in the last verse; that you willsell

yourself as a slave and yet no one will buy you.

People of God being blessed by God is not about praying or go to church neither declaring blessings, its about being OBEDIENT to His voice. Remember when Judah transgressed.

Do you have love and respect for people?

Respect for people is not just about being polite. It means honoring their ideas, values, privacy, and showing that you think they are worthy. These people can be your customers, friends, relatives, coworkers or your church's members. In whatever kind of relationship you're in, make sure you allow them to speak their minds and opinions.

When they talk, you listen and respond when they ask you something. It is all about being open minded.

You know, showing respect to other people is something that should be given freely. You don't sit quietly and suffer because you want to respect others, no, it's about respecting them on how they areand observe so you can raise a discussion on how you can help them if you found any issue or problem.

Listen! I am not here to push you to do something that you do not feel is right. If you really want to build and maintain good relationships, make more sales, and have a good reputation from others, follow these tips am about to share with you, and watch the results!

Be polite

Being polite to your customers is a sign of respect. Use "please" and "thank you" even for basic things. Hold doors open for people, offer to help your customers with anything they need. I'm using the term customers because those are the people I am dealing with every day. This tip can be applied to anybody that you associate with. It can be your parents, coworkers, and so on.

Never rebel against your customers.

There are people who know how to challenge you. If you happen to disagree with your customers or people around you, then do it in a very polite way. Ask them if you can talk with them in the office or privately. Present some clear and concise reasons why you disagree with them. Think of the consequences before you decide to make an argument. Also, collect as much information as you can because that if you look at that challenge in a positive way, it will help you to obtain a continuously improving business.

Read your customers mind

It's hard to be good to someone if you are not sure what they want from you or your company. Pay attention to what they are saying, because then you will know and be able to help by developing and proposing a solution. Your customers or staff make your business, without them you're nothing.

Formula 3
Opportunities

Let's see what it means when you hear the word "Opportunity".

From Collins dictionary; opportunity is a situation in which it is possible for you to do something that you want to do. Example: I had the opportunity to do business with the best actor in the world. Example: I had the opportunity to work with some doctor's or lawyer's office. Do you see that?

Identify the opportunities

Opportunity is always knocking at our door. The issue people have is knowing which opportunity to pursue and which ones to decline. Many of us struggling in this area whether we are men, women, entrepreneurs, or non entrepreneurs. We avoid allowing ourselves to jump into opportunities because we are afraid that we are going to lose our investments, instead of us looking in a great picture and finding a way to grow and develop ourselves and our business. I don't want to scare you or make you not think twice before you jump. No, what I am trying to share with you is, you have to think first before you take any action, but keep in mind, you do not need to be scared of any opportunities. Ok?

To be successful you need to be continually innovating and looking for opportunities to grow your business, project, or life. Don't be afraid to think outside the box when you're listing possible opportunities. You must understand, there's a difference between taking dangerous risks and calculated risks. Calculated risks involve knowing how you will receive a return. As a believer and entrepreneur, when we decide to create a business or expanding an established business, we have to do in God's way.

Utilize the Bible by following God's principles to create, expand, and maintain any business on this earth. Remember, our mind is the greatest gift God has given us and He expects us to use it in a way that will give Him glory.

How do you identify the opportunities?

- **Get advice from God** - God will speak to you about new opportunities, He knows our ends from the beginnings, He has experience and fulfills promises. God will reveal things to you that nobody would have done. Also, when God gives you an idea, He will put the tools and resources in your hands to make it happen. I love this God. Deuteronomy 28:12 says. "The Lord will open to you His good treasure, the heavens, to give the rain to your land in its season, and to bless all the work of your hand. You shall lend to many nations, but you shall NOT borrow."
- **Have an ear to listen** - Take time to listen to what others are saying about your industry, products, and services. This valuable information will help you identify key business opportunities to expand and develop your current products and services.
- **Find problems** - If you really want to start a business, the first thing you need to do is find the problem to solve.

Formula 4

Money

Save money

Saving money is not easy but God commands us to practice good financial stewardship in order to achieve our goals. We need to look at God's word and apply it in our life and our finances and ask God to teach us how to become faithful stewards in saving money. The Bible has so many verses that give wisdom about how to deal with our money and where to invest.

But let us talk about planning first, before we jump to the saving.

1 Timothy 6:17 "Teach those who are rich in this world not to be proud and not to trust in their money, which is so unreliable. Their trust should be in God, who richly gives us all we need for our enjoyment."

The Bible says; we have to put our Hope in God, but this doesn't mean that we shouldn't be planning ahead for the future, saving or investing. In fact, we are told that these are all wise things to do. The Bible makes it clear that it is wise to work hard and plan ahead for the future. Remember,

"If you fail to plan, you plan to fail, period."

Here are a few scriptures in the Bible talk about planning;

Luke 14:28-30 "Suppose one of you wants to build a tower. Won't you first sit down and estimate the cost to see if you have enough money to complete it? 29 For if you lay the foundation and are not able to finish it, everyone who sees it will ridicule you, 30 saying, 'This person began to build and wasn't able to finish.'

Proverbs 13:16 says; "A wise man thinks ahead; a fool doesn't, and even brags about it".

Proverbs 16: 9 In their hearts humans plan their course, but the LORD establishes their steps.

Proverbs 24:27 Prepare your work outside and make it ready for yourself in the field; afterwards, then, build your house.

Proverbs 12:15 The way of a fool is right in his own eyes, but a wise man listens to advice.

Proverbs 24:6 For by wise guidance you can wage your war, and in abundance of counselors there is victory.

Proverbs 6:6-8 Go to the ant, you sluggard; consider its ways and be wise! It has no commander, no overseer or ruler, yet it stores its provisions in summer and gathers its food at harvest.

Having a good plan frees you up to work smarter and helps you concentrate on the things that really matter to you.

Keep this in your mind, planning is key to success. If you do not have a plan for your life, then you will end up falling into someone else's plan and your life will end up in mediocrity lifestyle.

Saving and Investing

As I said before, saving is not easy, but we are commanded to do that in order to be ahead in the game of financial peace.

Saving up for a rainy day, putting your money to work, and multiplying it is a wise thing to do.

I have some scriptures to share with you that will help you to understand the importance of saving, investing, and change the way you manage your finances completely.

Matthew 25:14-30 *"For it is just like a man about to go on a journey, who called his own slaves and entrusted his possessions to them. To one he gave five talents, to another, two, and to another, one, each according to his own ability; and he went on his journey. Immediately the one who had received the five talents went and traded with them, and gained five more talents. In the same manner the one who had received the two talents gained two more. But he who received the one talent went away, and dug a hole in the ground and hid his master's money. Now after a long time the master of those slaves came and settled accounts with them. The one who had received the five talents came up and brought five more talents, saying, 'Master, you entrusted five talents to me. See, I have gained five more talents.' His master said to him, 'Well done, good and faithful slave You were faithful with a few things, I will put you in charge of many things; enter into the joy of your master.' Also the one who had received the two talents came up and said, 'Master, you entrusted two talents to me. See, I have gained two more talents.' His master said to him, 'Well done, good and faithful slave. You were faithful with a few things, I will put you in charge of many things; enter into the joy of your master.' And the one also who had received the one talent came up and said, 'Master, I knew you to be a hard man, reaping where you did not sow and gathering where you scattered no seed. And I was afraid, and went away and hid your talent in the ground. See, you have what is yours.' But his master answered and said to him, 'You wicked, lazy slave, you knew that I reap where I did not sow and gather where I scattered no seed. 'Then you ought to have put my money in the bank, and on my arrival I would have received my money back with interest. Therefore take away the talent from him, and give it to the one who has the ten talents.' For to everyone who has, more shall be given, and he will have an abundance; but from the one who does not have, even what he does have shall be taken away. Throw out the worthless slave into the outer darkness; in that place there will be weeping and gnashing of teeth."*

Genesis 41:34-36 Let Pharaoh appoint commissioners over the land to take a fifth of the harvest of Egypt during the seven years of abundance. They should collect all the food of these good years that are coming and store up the grain under the authority of Pharaoh, to be kept in the cities for food.

This food should be held in reserve for the country, to be used during the seven years of famine that will come upon Egypt, so that the country may not be ruined by the famine.

Proverbs 27:12 The prudent see danger and take refuge, but the simple keep going and pay the penalty.

Proverbs 30:24-25 Four things on earth are small, yet they are extremely wise: Ants are creatures of little strength, yet they store up their food in the summer.

Proverbs 21:20 The wise store up choice food and olive oil, but fools gulp theirs down.

Proverbs 21:5 The plans of the diligent lead to profit as surely as haste leads to poverty.

Look what Apostle Paul told Corinth church from the book of

1 Corinthians 16:2; "On the first day of every week, each one of you should set aside a sum of money in keeping with your income, saving it up, so that when I come no collections will have to be made."

In this scripture Apostle Paul was telling the Corinth church two things;

First, "to take up offerings before he arrives. When he arrives, he will help them route it to people in Jerusalem." Second, "he commanded them to set aside one day per week and give what they can." This was not a one-time offering. Instead, it was an ongoing, disciplined offering. So, what are we learning here?

In order to live in financial peace or financial prosperity as a child of

God, we must create smart ways to save our money;

1. Save Regularly– Just as Paul said in 1 Corinthians 16:2, it's better to save regularly instead of occasionally. If you can set up a system that will deduct money andsave aside do it now.
2. Save smart-No one of us knows what will happen from one day to the next, in our lives, so save big amount as much as you can instead of little amount is the way to go
3. Break the habits that keep you in debt, like spending more than you earn and borrowing. Save so you don't have to borrow.
4. Believe God's promise that your needs will be met.

——Diversify your money——

Equities are wonderful, but don't put all of your investment in one stock or one sector. None of us knows what will happen from one day to the next, in our lives and in the stock market. As a result, we are best served by diversifying our holdings to protect ourselves.

Let's look what bible say about diversify;

James 4:13-15 Now listen, you who say, "Today or tomorrow we will go to this or that city, spend a year there, carry on business and make money." Why, you do not even know what will happen tomorrow. What is your life? You are a mist that appears for a little while and then vanishes.

Instead, you ought to say, "If it is the Lord's will, we will live and do this or that."

Ecclesiastes 11:2 Invest in seven ventures, yes, in eight; you do not know what disaster may come upon the land.

———Be Faithful———

We're called on to be faithful and to deal justly. Invest ethically, and in a way that doesn't harm others. And here are scriptures to support this point;

Proverbs 28:20 A faithful man will abound with blessings, but he who makes haste to be rich will not go unpunished.

Proverbs 16:8 Better is a little with righteousness than vast revenues without justice.

Ecclesiastes 12:13 Now all has been heard; here is the conclusion of the matter: Fear God and keep his commandments, for this is the duty of all mankind.

Proverbs 13:11 Dishonest money dwindles away, but he who gathers money little by little makes it grow.

Something to keep in mind as you walk in your journey to your financial prosperity, God will multiply your finances when you surrender them fully to Him and to not allow money to be your ultimate goal. Instead, set your sights on Christ, make sure you pay your TENTH faithfully, then pay a close attention, you will notice that your money multiplies for reason you don't understand.

****

Proverbs 11:28

"He who trusts in his riches will fall, but the righteous shall flourish as the green leaf."

****

****

Remember, money is amoral, neither good or bad; how we handle it is the challenge.

****

Formula 5

Time

Invest Your Time Instead of Spending It

God's Word advises us to use our time wisely because He knows that there are many things in life that can distract us from what truly matters. Do not waste your time so that you look back with regret. Time is precious and it is important to keep in mind that you can't change the number of hours in a day, but you can fill them more efficiently. I have learned God's biblical principles on my way to becoming a financially free Christian, and I have seen how it has saved my life.

If you're serious about becoming financially free, take action and follow steps now:

1. Prioritize to focus on the most important tasks.
2. Make sure you're engaging in activities that support your business or project goals, both short- and long-term. I have seen many Christians waste oodles of time just because they're so easily distracted by multitasking. This is a big problem that makes worse for many of us. Instead of focusing on one task and finishing it in short order, we allow ourselves to be pulled off task numerous times. And this makes the original task takes much longer to finish.
3. Delegate tasks to others -These are the tasks that are urgent but not important or has a little value to your project or business.
4. Avoid unproductive meetings and conversations. You're the boss; do not hesitate to decline the request that are not important.
5. Limit your time on social media. It's easy to get trapped in a social media fall, where one profile leads to another and another. There's

a lot on the web to take your attention away from the important things in life. Don't let yourself be distracted. Set a daily limit to your social media use. I suggest that you follow fewer people on Facebook, Instagram, and other social media forums. This way there's less to consume.

6. Learn to finish the task You must know a key part to finishing is;
7. To make the decision that no matter what, this remaining task or project will remain no longer.
8. Make a plan of your task or project. You know you want to get some of your tasks completed, nothing else.
9. Make your deadlines.
10. Take note of what motivates you to complete tasks and projects. I believe that there's always ways to improve your ability to get things done by learning what is motivates you to run instead of walking.
11. Don't just finish, complete. Ask for support from professional people in that areas of your task or project, be patient, and keep positive attitude.
12. Become an expert in that area.
13. Treat yourself well. Make sure you get plenty of sleep, eat well (a balanced diet low in saturated and trans fats), and staying physically active. The study has shown; an alert mind is a high-functioning mind.

Here are the bible verses that talks about the importance of time:

2 Corinthians 6:2 "For he says, in the time of my favor I heard you, and in the day of salvation I helped you. I tell you, now is the time of God's favor, now is the day of salvation."

Ecclesiastes 3:11 "He has made everything beautiful in its time. He has also set eternity in the human heart; yet[a] no one can fathom what God has done from beginning to end."

Esther 4:14 "For if you remain silent at this time, relief and deliverance for the Jews will arise from another place, but you and your father's family will perish. And who knows but that you have come to your royal position for such a time as this?"

John 9:4 "As long as it is day, we must do the works of him who sent me. Night is coming, when no one can work."

Proverbs 16:9 "In their hearts humans plan their course, but the LORD establishes their steps."

Proverbs 27:1 "Do not boast about tomorrow, for you do not know what a day may bring."

Romans 13:11 "And do this, understanding the present time: The hour has already come for you to wake up from your slumber, because our salvation is nearer now than when we first believed."

Mark 13:32-33 "But about that day or hour no one knows, not even the angels in heaven, nor the Son, but only the Father. 33 Be on guard! Be alert! You do not know when that time will come."

Colossians 4:5-6 "5 Be wise in the way you act toward outsiders; make the most of every opportunity. 6 Let your conversation be always full of grace, seasoned with salt, so that you may know how to answer everyone"

1 Thessalonians 5:1-3 "Now, brothers and sisters, about times and dates we do not need to write to you, 2 for you know very well that the day of the Lord will come like a thief in the night. 3 While people are saying, "Peace and safety," destruction will come on them suddenly, as labor pains on a pregnant woman, and they will not escape."

Ephesians 5:15-17 "Be very careful, then, how you live, not as unwise but as wise, 16 making the most of every opportunity, because the days are evil.17 Therefore do not be foolish, but understand what the Lord's will is."

James 4:13-17 "13 Now listen, you who say, "Today or tomorrow we will go to this or that city, spend a year there, carry on business and make money."14 Why, you do not even know what will happen tomorrow. What is your life? You are a mist that appears for a little while and then vanishes. 15 Instead, you ought to say, "If it is the Lord's will, we will live and do this or that." 16 As it is, you boast in your arrogant schemes. All such boasting is evil. 17 If anyone, then, knows the good they ought to do and doesn't do it, it is sin for them."

Ecclesiastes 3:1-8 "1 There is a time for everything, and a season for every activity under the heavens: 2 a time to be born and a time to die, a time to plant and a time to uproot, 3 a time to kill and a time to heal, a time to tear down and a time to build, 4 a time to weep and a time to laugh, a time to mourn and a time to dance, 5 a time to scatter stones and a time to gather them, a time to embrace and a time to refrain from embracing, 6 a time to search and a time to give up, a time to keep and a time to throw away, 7 a time to tear and a time to mend, a time to be silent and a time to speak, 8 a time to love and a time to hate, a time for war and a time for peace."

"Do not waste your time so that you look back with regret."

Formula 6

Worth

You are Worthy

I want you to know that you are worthy and don't let your past to hold you back from moving forward. Your PAST has nothing to do with your life NOW. People's opinions have nothing to do with your future life, so start believing in yourself and do not allow people to take you away from what you know or what God has for you. God cares about our plans; He cares about our hearts too. He will never tell you to do anything that contradicts His Word.

By the way, I will advise you to eliminate negativity out of your life and cutting some people off. You have so much to do to reach your goals so there's no time to waste; only focus on positive things, things that will add value to your goals only.

Proverbs 14:7 says; "Stay away from a fool for you will not find knowledge on their lips"

A fool is unwise, lacks sense, and lacks judgement. Fools don't want to learn the truth. They laugh at the truth and turn their eyes away from the truth. Fools are wise in their own eyes failing to take in wisdom and advice, which will be their downfall. They suppress the truth by their unrighteousness. They have wickedness in their hearts, they are lazy, proud, they slander others, and live in repeat foolishness. Living in sin is fun for a fool. It's not wise to desire their company because they will lead you down a dark path. Fools rush into danger without wise preparation and thinking about the consequences. Scripture keeps people from being foolish, because who we surround ourselves with has a direct impact on our desire and ability to pursue the kind of life Jesus wants us to live. It is not possible to follow Him and ignore His warnings about people we should avoid. The friends we run closely with influence the direction we go in. If we want to be wise, we must surround ourselves with people who encourage us to make good decisions and help us avoid the deceit of foolishness.

You are not alone

Psalms 23:1-6 says, "1 The Lord is my shepherd, I lack nothing. 2 He makes me lie down in green pastures, he leads me beside quiet waters, 3 he refreshes my soul. He guides me along the right paths for his name's sake. 4 Even though I walk through the darkest valley,[a] I will fear no evil, for you are with me; your rod and your staff, they comfort me. 5 You prepare a table before me in the presence of my enemies. You anoint my head with oil my cup overflows. 6 Surely your goodness and love will follow me all the days of my life, and I will dwell in the house of the Lord forever."

Another scripture I like is from the book of Isaiah 41:10; fear not, for I am with you; be not dismayed, for I am your God; I will strengthen you, I will help you, I will uphold you with my righteous right hand.

When I think about of this promise that, "I am not alone," I am reminded that the grace of the Lord Jesus Christ and the love of God will sustain me and carry me through.

Formula 7

Purpose

Are you walking in your purpose or someone else's purpose?

We all have purpose; it is up to you to discover your purpose.

First, you need to understand this, your dream, your vision, or purpose is not for everyone so don't tell everybody everything unless God has allowed you to do so. You know when God gives us a vision or tells us to go and do something, the first thing we do is say I can't do that and give so many excuses. I am here to tell you today, stop making excuses! The best way to make progress is to START. Let go and let God!

Psalm 34:4; "I sought the Lord, and he answered me, he delivered me from all my fears."

What a blessing to be able to do the business or ministry that God directed you to do. If you believe and step out in faith, God will honor and bless you with the talent He has given you.

Most people wake up every day ONLY chasing other people's dream and they think they're in the right place.

Have you taken time to ask God, what is your purpose in this world? If the answer is YES, Kudos to you! If the answer is NO, then ask Him now. He will tell you.

Matthew 7:7 "Ask and it will be given to you; seek and you will find;

knock and the door will be opened to you."

You must have purpose in life because purpose is life. You cannot be without purpose. And the purpose becomes meaningful when you associate yourself with God, who will give you divine understanding, knowledge, and wisdom to carry it forth. God wants you to prosper as your soul prospers. He wants us to be rich.

Second question, did you know that God had already equipped you to carry out that purpose he showed you?

When you read at the book of Jeremiah 1:4-5 it says;

"The word of the Lord came to me, saying, Before I formed you in the womb I knew you, before you were born I set you apart; I appointed you as a prophet to the nations."

Look here, Not only did God know Jeremiah, but He chose him. Not only did God appoint Jeremiah, but He shaped him in his mother's womb. In the words of the Psalmist, we are "fearfully and wonderfully made" (Psalm 139:14). Jeremiah was set apart for a special purpose. The same words God told Jeremiah are the same words for me and all of you. God has special plans for everyone (Jeremiah 29:11-14). God has chosen us to do things and say things that will impact all time and eternity. I understand sometimes we get scared because the vision we are carrying can be big and we don't know where to start. When you try to reach out for advice maybe no one understands you, so it leads to fear, confusion, and wandering. In the end, it might lead you to the point of giving up or quitting completely. One thing you need to keep in mind is that not all spiritual leaders you know some with the big titles can lead you through your vision, purpose, or idea. Some may try to offer you their best advice to help to you, it may or may not work, not because they don't see as you see or feel as you feel. This vision is yours. It wasn't meant for them but for you. So if you're in that point now,

I want you to buckle up because we are going to fight with these types of devils called dream killers, delay, give up spirit, rejection, fear, manipulators, jealous, jezebel, spirit and so on. You need to be able to stand up tall and bold and make steps towards your purpose with confidence and assurance that God got your back. He is with you everywhere, He gave you a vision or talent, He will make sure He provides you with everything needed for you to start and run the race without turning back. He is able to do exceedingly, abundantly, and above all.

When God shows you your purpose and you have received confirmation that it is Him telling you to go start a business or nonprofit organization, you do not need to be scared of anything or anyone. You just need to trust Him and start your journey. I am not telling you something that I don't know. I am telling you the things that I've experienced myself and with the help of God I am here today because of my obedience to Him. Either people like you or not, support you or not, celebrate you or not. You need to learn to celebrate yourself and depend on Him 100%. He is a faithful God. If you walk according to His word, anything He said to you through dreams, prophecies, or revelation, will come to pass no matter how long it will take. The bible says, our God is not human, that he should lie, not a human being, that he should change his mind.

You know, being human we forget many things oftentimes because that's our nature to forget. This really reminds me of when I was giving birth to my firstborn. I told my mom that "this one child is enough mama no more, that's it." My mom laughed so hard and said to me, "My daughter, do not say this to other people, because within no time you will find yourself pregnant and so excited to welcome your second child." And that is exactly what happened lol! As I matured in this, I began to encourage and inspire new moms by letting them feel comfortable and familiarize themselves with this new life.

Back to our topic, no matter how many times you receive rejection and discouragement from people, remember one thing, it's not over until God say it's over. Keep thriving, keep pushing, your destiny helpers or help will be few steps away. I am speaking about the God I know, the God whose power I have testified of. He is a covenant keeping God. Philippians 1:6 says, "being confident of this, that he who began a good work in you will carry it on to completion until the day of Christ Jesus."

Jeremiah revealed to God his fear of rejection because of his youth. Timothy had the same problem. Paul instructed him not to let anyone despise his youth, but instead, to be an example to believers in speech, conduct, love, faith, and purity (1 Timothy 4:12). Look this! God declared to Jeremiah that he would go to everyone God sent him to, speak whatever God told him to speak, and not to fear anyone. Because He is with him and he promised to deliver him. When you're continuing to read the book of Jeremiah you will see the Bible says, "Jeremiah responded in faith." He went to everyone to whom God sent him and spoke everything God said. As God, indeed, was with Jeremiah, He will be with you to carry out His purpose.

A very important thing that you need to know is, you must acknowledge your purpose and know that, He is with you all the way and has equipped you to carry out His purpose. Your help is coming from Him and no one else. He will send ravens to feed you as he did to His Servant Elijah from the book of 1 Kings 17:1-7. Maybe you have people in your life trying to tell you different from what God has shown you or telling you. You need to stay away from those people from now on. I call them dream killers and manipulators. They are pretending to know you and what God has for you better than anybody. My dear friend, "What are you waiting for? RUN!!!" These people will kill your dreams and ideas. You will find yourself stuck in one place, no progress, always complaining or as I like to say, "singing the song with the same melody." Be angry for change, demand your space, resist the devil, and he will flee away from you. It really is that simple. God knows you and claims to know you. Nothing makes a person feel better than to be known by someone who is a BIG shark, so STOP walking on other people's purpose. Start walking in your own purpose.

Don't allow yourself to be a slave anymore! Take time to ask God anything that you need Him to show to you. He will show you and teach you things that nobody else can. He will direct your steps, but the thing is, He is waiting for you to take a step of faith and act.

Then, go again to God and tell Him to bless you so you can walk in your purpose with all blessings of Abraham, Isaac, and Jacob. The bible is full of examples of people who went to Jesus for a blessing or touch. Apart from Jesus, we can do nothing that matters (John 15:5). That is why we need to be equipped by God to do our task. His touch enables us and empowers us to carry out our purpose.

Remember, your task is to discover God's will for your life and to do it.

Investing in Your Purpose

The purpose of investing is to see something tangible happen or something get birth out of your purpose. Let me tell you, when you know your purpose, investing in it comes so easily. You do not need somebody to push or remind you, you just decide in your mind that "I will commit to my purpose until something happens."

The reason many people's purpose, hopes, and dreams don't come to life, don't last longer or die premature death, is because of being surrounded with bad people or advisors, they don't want to see anything good comes from you, they want to see you remain behind while they move forward. They see you trying to invest into your purpose still they never leave you alone.

Listen, your work is not to listen to those people, your role is to commit to your purpose and make sure you bring all of it into the world, not half of it, all that was given to you by God. If it's to cut sleep instead of sleeping 9 hours, sleep 4-5 hours for the sake of your vision. If it is to save money so you can expand your business or start one, do it now. Try to do all the possible things, so God can do the impossible things for you. He is a way maker. He will make a way where seems to be no way.

Work Hard and Work Smart

God's words tell us that working hard, but with faith in mind, can lead to the great things he has planned for us. If you read Colossians 3:23 says,

"Whatever you do, work at it with all your heart, as working for the Lord, not for human masters"

Also, from the book of Proverbs 27:23-27 says;

23 Be sure you know the condition of your flocks, give careful attention to your herds; 24 for riches do not endure forever, and a crown is not secure for all generations. 25 When the hay is removed and new growth appears and the grass from the hills is gathered in, 26 the lambs will provide you with clothing, and the goats with the price of a field. 27 You will have plenty of goats' milk to feed your family and to nourish your female servants.

These verses are encouraging us to work hard and smart, It does not matter what type of business you own or doing, large or small,

Solomon tells us, it is important and our responsibility to use those blessings of crops and vineyards -not to let them go to waste.

God has given all of us talents that we can sell, but that doesn't mean you should start a business, project or ministry right away. Instead make yourself a student of what you want to do, first. Then, make sure there's a paying client or supporter for your product or service. Finally, develop your business and leadership skills so that you can turn your talent into a real deal(business).

Proverbs 10:4 “Lazy hands make for poverty, but diligent hands bring wealth”.

Let’s read Proverbs 6:6-11: (Be Wise in Your Work Ethic)

6 Go to the ant, you sluggard; consider its ways and be wise! 7 It has no commander, no overseer or ruler, 8 yet it stores its provisions in summer and gathers its food at harvest. 9 How long will you lie there, you sluggard? When will you get up from your sleep? 10 A little sleep, a little slumber, a little folding of the hands to rest—11 and poverty will come on you like a thief and scarcity like an armed man.

Solomon used an excellent example of a good work ethic,the ant. The ant does not have to have someone pushing it to do what it knows it has to do. It gathers and prepares for the winter. Farmers do the same thing. We, as humans, need to do the same thing better than the ant. We must develop the habit of work smart and save for what we want so we don’t worry about paying back.

“The vision God gave you is not for everyone, was made special for you so stop to make everyone involved.”

Formula 8

Celebration

Celebrate Other People's Achievements.

Achieving success is something that practically all of us strive for. We want to achieve our goals and see our dreams become reality. We need to create a culture of celebrating other people's success when we do that, we release the glory of God in our life. God wants us to love and honor one another.

In John 13:34 Jesus taught, "A new command I give you: Love one another. As I have loved you, so you must love one another." Then He added, "By this everyone will know that you are my disciples, if you love one another" (verse 35).

Look at the book of Romans 12:15, "Rejoice with those who rejoice, weep with those who weep." Apostle Paul tells us we MUST rejoice with those who rejoice. Jesus displayed His remarkable ability to empathize with the condition of His people during His earthly ministry. He wept at the tomb of His friend Lazarus (John 11:28–35). There is no doubt, Jesus felt the pain over what the people thought would be a permanent loss of life. But because of the Power and Love He carried, He was able to bring back His friend Lazarus.

Since Jesus could mourn with those who mourn, we also know that He can rejoice with those who rejoice. Let us learn from Jesus example to be a good servant who emphasizes with others while remaining angry toward sin, who finding a way to bring joy and a positive energy everywhere we go, let us love one another, for love comes from God. Everyone who loves has been born of God and knows God.

This is a question to ask ourselves, how do we feel when a friend or family member won something they craved to have? Do we celebrate or do we hate? Well, without doubt, we should be happy.

If you're having difficulty rejoicing with another, first of all, I'm asking you to "Repent" of such attitudes and ask God to help you learn to rejoice truly with other, because that attitude is not coming from Him.

Second, we need to evaluate ourselves and our relationship with them. It is my belief that when you care about someone and want to maintain positive relationships with them, it means that we have their best interest at heart. If so, then cheering their accomplishments become so easy. The core of our relationship should surpass any element of jealous or concern.

From my journey of becoming a successful person inside and out, I've learnt so many things. One of the things I learned was to find a way that can motivate me to have a healthy and well-balanced relationship.

I started to brainstorm on how to naturally celebrate other people success even when I don't feel like it. I do understand the process of waiting for your breakthrough can be overwhelming sometimes but trust me your time will come. By the way, who knows? Maybe you're the next in the line. Always trust the process and trust the Lord (God).

Here are some good tips I have come up with, to show you why we need to celebrate other people's achievements. I am sure when you apply these tips you will truly start to see a big change in your relationship with others

1. We need each other to succeed -We truly need healthy and friendly competition that will make each other to push harder but you must make sure it doesn't turn to jealousy.
2. It motivates us to drive for our personal success when you have friends or family members who have climbed the mountain before you, it's a good thing because they will be your role models, you

will be able to learn from them and life becomes so easy.

3. It shows that you care about the person -When you love and care about someone, you will always want to see them succeed. You will never want to see them fail or fall short of their goals .

Continue to walk in God's Abundant life with gratitude.

I'm so grateful the God we serve is a God of abundance—

Jesus said in John 10:10, "I have come that they may have life, and have it to the full."

God is a God who lives in our day to day, granting us new mercies and new blessings every day. We have to learn to trust God as Jehovah-Jireh—our faithful Provider and thank Him for everything.

Your key to overflowing abundance has nothing to do with your abilities or on the economic systems of this world. Your breakthrough will come from looking to the Lord and trusting Him to do what only He can do! The psalmist says this well: "Unto You I lift up my eyes, O You who dwell in the heavens" (Psalm 123:1).

Do you know the more you set your heart on the Lord God, the more you will experience the joy and peace of overflowing abundance in His presence and His provision?

"Remember, by rejoicing with other people, we show our love for them in Christ."

ACKNOWLEDGMENTS

SPECIAL THANKS TO MY HUSBAND for supporting me and my dreams. What an amazing husband!

Also, thanks to my biological sister Aika Abisay for always standing with me in prayer and encouraging me. You are special to me.

And to my dear friend Dr. Baptiste, thank you for your kindness and unconditional support. You are truly a great friend.

Mom & Dad, thank you for your love and teaching me what books couldn't; you are the best parents in the world.

ABOUT THE AUTHOR

Veronica Swai would be described as a wife, a mother of 3 kids, an entrepreneur and a minister of the gospel. The Lord Jesus Christ is her Savior and MASTER of her life.

She realized her purpose when she had her personal encounter with Jesus Christ of Nazareth. Her mission is to share the gospel, inspire, empower, and motivate YOU to be the BEST person that God has created you to be spiritually, physically, mentally and financially.

www.ingramcontent.com/pod-product-compliance
Lightning Source LLC
Chambersburg PA
CBHW070638150426
42811CB00050B/379
9781733805179